UPDATE

Also by Dennis O'Driscoll

Dennis O'Driscoll

Update

POEMS 2011–2012

Copper Canyon Press
Port Townsend, Washington

Cover art: Patrick Scott, Untitled from *Meditations,* 2007, carborundum with gold leaf, edition of 50, 60 × 60 cm. Courtesy of the artist's estate and Taylor Galleries, Dublin.

Copper Canyon Press is in residence at Fort Worden State Park in Port Townsend, Washington, under the auspices of Centrum. Centrum is a gathering place for artists and creative thinkers from around the world, students of all ages and backgrounds, and audiences seeking extraordinary cultural enrichment.

LIBRARY OF CONGRESS CATALOGING-IN-PUBLICATION DATA

O'Driscoll, Dennis.
[Poems. Selections]
Update / Dennis O'Driscoll.
pages ; cm
ISBN 978-1-55659-484-7 (pbk. : alk. paper)
I. Title.
PR6065.D75A6 2015
821'.914--dc23
2015012507

3 5 7 9 8 6 4 2
FIRST PRINTING

Copper Canyon Press
Post Office Box 271
Port Townsend, Washington 98368

www.coppercanyonpress.org

ACKNOWLEDGMENTS

Publisher's note adapted from a version by Peter Jay of Anvil Press Poetry.

'Gallery Nude' was written for the National Gallery of Ireland for an anthology for their 150th Anniversary in 2014.

'Then' was published in January 2014 in *The Irish Times.*

'Update' was published in 2013 by *Poetry Ireland Review.*

Thanks to J. Patrick Lannan and the Lannan Foundation (New Mexico) for their support while Dennis was working on these poems.

CONTENTS

PUBLISHER'S NOTE

AFTER the completion of *Dear Life,* his ninth collection of poems, Dennis O'Driscoll kept his finished manuscripts in a computer file titled "Newest Poems." This collection was twice subtitled: "Since completion of *Dear Life*" and "April 2011–." The file was last modified two days before his death on Christmas Eve 2012.

This book reproduces that file unchanged. It is certain that Dennis would have not only added more poems but also prepared the collection for publication with his customary attention and care in arrangement.

He had already been thinking about possible titles for a book, but none of the half-dozen phrases he jotted down comes from these finished poems. The title was chosen by his wife, Julie O'Callaghan, in cooperation with his British publisher, Peter Jay of Anvil Press Poetry.

Despite the collection's provisional nature, these are poems that all of Dennis O'Driscoll's readers will want to have. Although Dennis would have worked toward perfection, what you hold is perhaps not far short of being a completed collection—and very much in line with his previous books. Darker even than much of *Dear Life,* still the poems are full of his inimitable humor, earnest curiosity, and characteristic wit and wisdom.

UPDATE

THE ROCKS

The rocks are determined
to spend each second well.
They calculate on a geologic
scale the time they can still

reckon on, and have no
expectation of escaping
the sun's blowout, predicted
in a mere five billion years.

Stoically, they hold their nerve,
adapt calmly to their limited prospects,
expand or contract as each
season's heat or cold demands.

Intent on making the best
of things, they treat each day
as though it were the last, use
their time enjoyably while they may.

They will be dust long enough.

TICKING THE BOXES

Tick the relevant boxes
in this census form tonight
if you are still in the land
of the living at that time.
You must remain
in suspense until then.

You have all morning still.
You have all afternoon long.
One continuous hour.
A whole six minutes.
Twenty-eight precious seconds left.
Three.
Two.
One.

In which to lose your job.
Your citizenship.
Your house.
Your spouse.
Your child.
Your mind.
Your sight.
Your faith.
Your life.

Count on absolutely nothing yet.

STREETWISE

Do I what?
Of course. Of course.
I know him all too well.
We keep on bumping into one another,
me and that agitated man –
semblance, soul brother –
who mutters to himself at all hours
as he roams the streets,
comfortless in his own skin,
clearly a seasoned hand
at the contrition game,
in the advanced stages
of self-reprimand,
driven to taking disadvantage
of himself, vandalising his mind,
attempting a citizen's self-arrest,
staging a public show trial,
engaging in *ad hominem* accusations,
adducing self-incriminating evidence.

Settling old scores,
he practises own goals
compulsively, penalty kicks,
has them down to an art
as fine as the sword on which
a broken man will fall.

A middle of the night waker,
no doubt, tireless in his rigorous
self-appraisal; unable to mediate
a peace in the protracted stand-off
between self and self, hostilities

raging on both sides of his divide.
He is his own worst enemy.

Then the silent treatment begins:
no longer on speaking terms with himself,
he serves a barring order on his person,
wondering which – if any – of his selves
he should seek custody of.

Even in seemingly quietist phases,
his somnambulist's gait
gives his game away.
Scratched eyes. Contorted face.
How, without forewarning,
he lashes out suddenly,
lunging at some nobody
down a solitary dead-end.

BIG APPLE

bistros buffets
burger joints
brasseries
eat all you can
low-cal
fat-free
supersize
jumbo
triple scoop
club
dagwood
drive-thru
take-out
chrome-trim vintage diners
glinting through the night
greasy spoons
members-only clubs
farm-fresh wild tenderised
macrobiotic organic vegan green
fillet of supreme of cream of
puree prime-cut lean
tear and share
house specials
catch of the day
belly dancer singing waiter karaoke cabaret
delis where money can buy you anything
milk and honey
manna and ambrosia
house-smoked peppery pastrami
with asiago cheese on rye
spicy cilantro-marinated swordfish
cedar-wrapped ginger squash salmon
McDonald's Pizza Hut Dunkin Donuts KFC

O brave New World
that offers such abundance
O land of the free the obese the anorexic the bulimic
the morning-after lycra-clad joggers
strapped to heart monitors pedometers
protein drinks in holsters

spring sunshine reinvigorates the lunchtime park
at which office workers unlatch sushi boxes
fork tuna salads from their screwtop plastic bowls

lunch is a legitimate business expense
for the executives who don their Gucci specs
to scrutinise the wine list
in the Michelin-starred penthouse
while the bowtied sommelier
keeps his discreet counsel
until vouchsafed a peremptory nod

so much unfailing comfort to avail of
at the food bar where singles
ladle ready-meals for dinner
curried wheatberry salad lemon mint
citrus kamut chicken enchilada
orzo with olives edamame succotash
such a glut that surplus tons
are slopped out nightly into trash bins

next stop the gym
to work off excess cals
manipulate weights at muzak tempo
hasten to the treadmill's measured destination
man – like galley slaves – the rowing machines
resolve to test the latest low-carb diet
no greater terror to war against
than the sight of the accusatory

bathroom scales gaining ground
advancing like the hands
of the doomsday nuclear clock

halal kosher fast food slow
peeled prepared cleaned
julienned dressed sliced diced
seasoned stuffed marinated
traceable sustainable fairtrade
squeezed plucked rolled boned
smoked crowned skewered rotisseried
halved quartered drawn BBQ-ed
skimmed raw fortified with vitamins iron
microwavable suitable for freezing just add water

a people content to live with blueberry smoothies
bircher muesli soaked overnight in yoghurt
leek and pea risotto with grilled calamari
dreamy cream-filled cupcakes
chocolate malted crunch hand-scooped ice cream shake
prime T-bone onion rings hash browns
tempura-battered Chicken McNuggets
chinese cabbage tofu soup

wars fought in their names
are tucked safely out of sight
like the faceless illegals
who pick on asparagus tips
bow low in heat
to rows of big-hearted lettuces
frilled as the bathing costume of a paddling child
cooling off blissfully in her backyard pool

no need at all to soil your hands
unless they smudge on Belgian chocolate muffins
contract a tincture of the sticky spare-rib sauce

no antibiotic no growth hormone no gluten
no added sugar sodium no artificial flavours
no dairy no transfats no synthetic colours
no emulsifiers no bad carbs no MSG no 'E's

no issues no sweat
nothing whatsoever to fret about
worry yourself sick over
health inspectorate
food and drugs administration
biodegradable packaging
carbon write-offs making reparation
for refrigerated truck deliveries
guilty air miles
peace and plenty
and lots lots more where all that came from
everything *everything* to go

ESCAPISM

Even without these shoes, they would have tramped home happily on bare soles: a ragged army in triumphal march, so much did they miss their little shtetls.

Even without these metal prostheses, even without these crutches, they would eventually have limped to the finishing lines of their village squares, where dogs still kept expectant vigils, chickens picked their broody way through cobbles.

Even without their bales of hair, the houseproud women would have beamed as brightly as the full moon's candid stare through newly-fitted window panes.

Even without these suitcases, they would have gladly sent themselves packing, to rebuild the ghettoes with fired brick, secure the picket boundaries around their intimate Jerusalems.

Even without their teeth, they would have eaten heartily, treated each mushy dish as a Passover feast.

Even without these glasses, they would have tracked their way back by blind instinct, recited the joyful hallel psalms by rote.

Even without these canisters of gas, they would have died in the fullness of time, reunited with their bedside children, buried with full honours by grown sons.

Auschwitz Museum

And when, inevitably, the liquidator moves in, pushes you aside, convenes a meeting of your fretful creditors, you must seize the initiative at once, get your PR team cracking on communiqués for immediate release, putting a positive spin on your actions.

Learn to say you fell victim to a global downturn, stiff competition from the East, soaring labour costs, crippling taxation, unfavourable exchange rates, excessive regulation and compliance requirements – red tape gone mad – not to mention insufficient vigilance of cowboy operators, cack-handed official crackdowns on the black economy. Reel off, too, some spiel about decline in discretionary spending, shifting tastes, migration online of your dwindling customer base, the market flooded with cheap counterfeits. Slip in climate change. Commodity price hikes. The unreliability of raw material supplies from war zones.

Save face. Persuade acquaintances you've flourished in adversity. Bang on about a learning curve, the premium you place now on your cherished family and friends, enjoying quality time with your partner, assisting your kids with school assignments, life-work balance perfectly in sync.

Lay it on the line about your struggle, day and night, to save the business, slaving only for the taxman in the end, crippled by bank interest, the cash-flow tap turned off, ineligible for further subsidies or grants. Reference the effects of chronic stress. The health toll.

Or, with a mischievous smirk, shoot the breeze with drinking pals about the liabilities you've parked, jettisoned for others to worry over. And, lest debt collecting agencies or Revenue investigators home in uncomfortably close, you've made sure to shred sensitive records, stash vulnerable assets offshore.

Publicly, speak of failure as a badge of courage; at least you had the guts to try. Quote that witty quip you heard at Rotary: '... something ... something ... fail again better'.

It never hurts – voice quaking with emotion – to bullshit about some cod addiction: alcohol, online gambling, say. Depression hits the spot too. Steer well clear of cocaine. If more desperate measures are called for, be seen to sign into a clinic; play along with counselling until the storm has safely passed.

Always stonewall awkward questioners by reference to legal proceedings pending. You are precluded from comments that might prejudice the outcome of a trial. Your thoughts at this time are with your loyal staff.

And, needless to add, in cases tainted with a hint of impropriety, allegations of hanky-panky carry-on with employees, you must take the tried-and-trusted route of an ancillary statement from your spouse, a carefully-slanted declaration of the standing-by-you kind, the sort that pleads for privacy at this – what's the phrase again? – this *difficult time* for you and your family.

Express regret only insofar as absolutely necessary; even then, confine remorse within the narrowest parameters, lest you come across as wimpish, weak. Vaguely allude to possible new ventures in the pipeline. A clean slate. Maintain an option on name-checking God.

THEN

Hard though I know
you find this to believe,
I was actually alive once.
Alive. And well enough,
at least, to play my part.

I too faced heartaches, disappointments,
embarrassments and vanities
not all that unlike yours, kept up
with the pressing issues of the day,
registered weather's moodiness

on my skin, brooded on the big
life-and-death questions when
I indulged my more reflective traits.
And if it's any consolation,
it feels no less strange to me now

to conceive that I was truly
such a creature once,
and had some small say in how
the world – as it stood at that
time – conducted its affairs.

That my birth would not make
a blind bit of difference,
in the final analysis, does not
negate my life, and counts
for precious little against

the surges of unbounded joy
I felt, on better days, imagining
my highest hopes were still fulfillable.
There was everything to live for then.
It was all before me.

BORN FREE

We have been rumbled, unmasked,
shown up for what we really are,
reduced to our blood-and-water essence,
confirmed to be a cocktail of amino
acid sequences, interacting proteins,
myosin, insulin, enzymes and all
the well-documented elements
that serve as our nerve-wired contrivance,
our millennia-aged behaviour
still dictated by the same old trite
devices, manipulated by their primitive
bag of hackneyed tricks.

We are standard models, economy stock,
our systems equipped with similar
connective tissue, acting out –
to the last chromosomal cue –
the genome's encoded script,
not one among us capable of reasoning
for himself, every thought emerging
from the regulation synapses, every task
we undertake a reflex to some hoary
neural stimulus, a kneejerk reaction
to primal cognitive commands.

What gets you down is not your son's
accidental death, your acrimonious divorce,
but your crying need for a top-up of serotonin.
Blood sugar and hormone levels determine
the vicissitudes of your daily moods.
Prayers and swear words issue through
likeminded channels of brain tissue;

an equivalent succession of cortex processes
heralds an act of magnanimity or rape.
No better than the sum of our corporeal
parts, it seems, our heartfelt professions
of love are revealed to be the cunning ruse
of androgens to achieve their devious goals.

Plot as commonplace as the monotonous course
our oxygenated blood constantly adopts, we are
an open book, exposed to the close-reading
of a microscopic eye: a crow's intrusive scrutiny
of a hedgehog's gory entrails, its inside story.

AMOK

You feed your inner demon
with the prime cuts of your life,

fatten it, a hand-raised hog,
throw it your juiciest scraps,

let it run loose among
your private grounds.

*

Sniffing around whatever
chestnuts you've concealed,

it unearths secreted kernels,
starts squealing indiscreetly

on you, brings pungent
truffles to the surface.

*

Exposing your most tender
roots, it wallows in the mud

it stirs up, proves capable
of making it stick.

Your heart is in its mouth now,
your future in its cloven hooves.

TODODAY

Distance is the soul of beauty.
– SIMONE WEIL

How will this seemingly off-the-rack day
eventually stack up? A day that does
its routine duty, and is pulling out
the stops now for the usual grand finale,
as the sun, voyage terminating, discharges
runny colours like ship's bilge.

Will this day survive the test of time?
Will we live to see it notch up classic rating,
like a novel – posthumously acclaimed –
that had suffered multiple rejections,
a reappraised basement painting
newly accorded old master status?

Could this day – so humdrum it seems
forgettable – become numbered among
our very best: free of crisis, a vindication
of the quiet life; belated recognition for
an understated Sunday that shunned
the limelight, yet may still withstand scrutiny?

Might what appeared, in its own day,
to have made a modest splash, at most,
seem nearly faultless in a retrospective light,
redeem the reputation days gain for adversity,
shine sublimely in past tense, display
an unsuspected aptitude for happiness?

TRUCE

I have no idea what came over me.
It was so totally out of character.

Stand-offish – hostile even – though
I'd learned to be, I embraced myself
unwarily for once, renewed acquaintance,
blurted out a few supportive words,
enquired if I might help with anything,
plumped my pillow, dabbed my forehead,
gave me as much encouragement as I could.

I just cannot for the life of me imagine
what sparked off that rapprochement.
But I was glad we had laid down our arms.
It was exactly like old times, when me and I
were constant comrades, trusted buddies:
at ease in our own presence,
able to bear the other's company, enjoy
a no-holds-barred, heart-to-heart confab.

It was as if I recognised
this final chance for what it was.
As if I'd had some tip-off
about not seeing myself again.

NEW YEAR PARTY

By landslide vote
we drive the old year out,
unanimously pass
motions of no confidence.

It had been granted an entire year
to fulfil its promise, only to renege
on its mandate, plague the world
sadistically with tribulation.

The new year's manifesto
is progressive, forward looking.
Now we may turn a fresh leaf,
happy that winter's recession
will give way to steady growth,
longer, balmier, user-friendly days.

We take to the streets:
rabid supporters of the New Year
party, cheering its inauguration,
determined to renew its mandate
annually from now on.

Let the midnight countdown begin.
High time the bells chimed
with our boisterous rejoicing,
lent ringing endorsement
to our future prospects,
while last year's absolute ruler
is banished: Disgraced.
Outdated. Past it. History.

COMEDY

We have worked through most of life's
set-pieces now, assumed the roles of mewling
infant, truant student, canteen-fed breadwinner,
toothless, treble-voiced old codger.

Our 'exeunt all' phase is advancing:
the finale where the circling actors
dance their hearts out and the spirited
veterans earn a special round of cheers.

The wise old couple, the pair who
spared the king's abandoned child,
rise to the occasion, kicking up their heels,
ceasing for the moment to act their age.

*

Lower the curtain while the going is
still good, and all the world's this stage,
while, fresh from solemn vows, the starry-eyed
newlyweds take their prolonged bows.

Nothing ill will happen while the dancing
lasts, while the enchanted audience claps time
to galliards and the tambourine-jingling
jester leads the rhythmic yelps and hups.

Bring down the curtain quickly, like a vinyl
privacy screen around a hospice bed.
Make no further scenes. Give no intimation
of what, ever after, takes place next.

THE MAIN EVENT

We frittered away so much of life
organising our lives –
scraping a minimal wage,
meeting household outgoings,
grappling with family demands –
we lost track of whatever it was
we were supposed to be alive for.

There was something about life
that resisted living, put itself on
the long finger continually,
lent precedence to the mundane tasks
that needed immediate attention,
so that we never quite got to the point.

Outmanoeuvred at every step,
hampered in our efforts to participate,
frustrated like snubbed customers,
closing time drinkers who failed
to catch the barman's eye,

we missed out on the main event,
rising each day to find
what diversions were lined up
that would delay us ever longer
from making life's acquaintance.

BREVIARY

Summer

The pickaxe plop
of a lobbed-back shot
all summer from
the tennis club.

*

Dinner

a woman in kitchen mitts
pounces like a boxer

summons her tardy
children from the garden

challenges them
to step inside

*

Blackrock Clinic

You take a turn:
the second left
after Ben Inagh Park.

*

Postcard from Tiberias

Sun brings out
    the Sea of Galilee
in pure azure.

On a clear day
    you can see
God from here.

*

1959

Best of all treats for the feverish
young patient: luminescent grapes,
pearls of great price for which
straitened parents sacrificed.

Fork out for a bunch in Bertie's
and he'd automatically enquire
'Who's sick?', then fling
an extra fistful in the bag.

Get Well gesture.
Corporal work of mercy.
Cure for whatever ails you.
Just what the doctor ordered.

*

Magpies

Magpies curse you from a height,
fly off with scoffing sounds
when their protection racket is disturbed.

*

House of the Dead

A day of ashen silence,
an icy chapel of rest.

Below leafless trees
with skeletal nests,

'wreaths of smoke'
heave from

a grief-choked
chimney breast.

*

The Accident

Had you spent a split second less at A.
Had you delayed an extra minute at B.

Had you hesitated before entering C.
Had you been a tad more cautious at D.

Had you bided your time at E.
Had you changed your mind before settling on F.

Had you clawed that accidental moment back.
Had you been given – A to Z – your life to live all over again.

*

Floods

Water under the bridge
flows from the tears of those
who cried their eyes out
over spilt milk.

*

End of Term

students at
the University of Life
we await our final grades

still ignorant
of how we
were appraised

no wiser
as to who it was
that set the tests

in the dark
about what
marks success

*

Taking Your Life

I know where
     you are
coming from.

But not where
     you will take
your only life.

*

Honoris Causa

Your last honorary degree
     will be an R.I.P.
conferred posthumously.

FAME

The bells your
name once rang
no longer toll,
their clappers
fallen silent.

FLIES

The flies of today
are no longer the flies of yore
– RAYMOND QUENEAU

No, they don't make flies
    like they used to anymore:
big bruisers with limber wings,
    fidgety legs kicking
germs in your face,
    capable of dismembering
a brace of roadkill rodents
    in a single, sated morning,
swarming to the crash scene
    like emergency services,
or slurping a drunk's
    hurtled spillage
while still appetisingly warm.
    Exemplary team workers,
they set contentedly about
    their tasks, humming
at their toil, rebuffing
    the distraction of
a baton-wielding fly conductor
    when they made landfall
on a butcher's luscious bloodbath,
    hygienically dispensed
with a load of roadside crap,
    or pressed a viral gift
on some unsuspecting
    beneficiary's kitchen.
Such hefty specimens
    there were in olden times,
a far cry from the scrawny
    pushovers of today.

A pleasure to behold:
     strapping, brassy chaps
with healthy all-you-can-eat
     mentalities, hatched out
on squelchy cowpats,
     flexing wrestlers' pecs
before a round or two
     of jousting with
pavement café diners,
     then cooling off in
soothing sirloin juices,
     backstroking a few lengths
in the deep end of a wound.
     We miss them bitterly
when summer comes,
     how they swooped down
like clouds of sticky heat,
     creating a lively buzz,
always good for a laugh,
     hassling cattle, battling
campsite picnickers,
     making a pass at lovers
supine in a fragrant hayfield,
     teasing listless sheep.
So unlike the gutless types
     in circulation nowadays,
prim, figure-conscious snobs,
     all skinny limbs, manicured nails;
failing to meet their quotas
     in the salmonella department,
remiss about dysentery dispersal,
     tolerating deficiencies
in cholera dissemination,
     proffering pesticide-based
excuses for their lack of breeding,
     a flyweight disgrace

to their species, betraying
        the heritage of brave forebears:
gallant freedom fighters,
        front-line combatants
against oppression by flypapers,
        spiderwebs and sprays.
Conscientious messengers,
        they conveyed first-hand
news of fashionable
        pathogens to die for,
gorgeous wings as glossy
        as a corpse's suppurations,
a pony's running sores.

LUNCHTIME

And yet, for all that you are
technically dead for decades,
certified as such in public records,
I know otherwise.
Only today I watched you
venture out in your paisley-patterned
crossover apron, elastic stockings,

bearing the good tidings
of your straw shopping bag
past the box hedge, wasp-pocked
orchard, heavy-lidded rose beds,
tenebrous sheds of sows,
suckler cows, deep-litter hens,
then face the full glare

of the unsparing sun
in light-headed meadows
basking on grass mats,
to find that the hay-saving men
are gagging for a sup of 'tay',
tongues 'hanging out
with the drought'.

And here you are,
now and forever,
unpacking the vacuum flask,
the luncheon meat sandwiches,
the newly-baked caraway cake,
the sugar-studded rhubarb pie,
the enamel mugs,

giving the lie to those
who gave you up for dead.

THE GOOD OLD DAYS

*'The music of what happens', said great Fionn, 'that is the finest
music in the world.'*

— THE FENIAN CYCLE

And did his warriors not go on
to ask Fionn what the saddest music is?

I catch an old-style sing-song from
my Alzheimer neighbour's house.

She is home for Christmas,
her family have gathered in her name.

They chat about times past,
look back on her behalf to happy days.

Maybe Fionn's response was, 'The music
of yearning: that is the saddest music in the world.'

They press on with their reminiscing,
then launch into a further bygone number.

They do this in remembrance of her.

OBIT

Like all the mothers round the town,
ours was shamelessly immodest
when it came to talking up her children:
their roles in carol concerts, school plays;
their end-of-term reports; their drollery,
their funny deeds; the glorious careers
they would be guaranteed.

Now is our chance to do her
proud, in turn, show her to full
advantage, keep her memory alive.
How best to set about the task?
We can't very well mention her
prowess with soda bread; it had
to be savoured – steaming hot,
nut-flavoured, streaming
buttery rivulets – to be believed.
And her pièces de résistance –
the sherry trifle after Sunday lunch,
the flawless cherry cakes in which
the fruit never clustered at the base –
were scarcely the stuff of newspapers,
even those where anything local goes.

Where did this leave her? Or us?
We checked the previous issue's
obits for 'housewife' write-ups.
All were reportedly of 'quiet,
unassuming disposition' – one
with a weakness for bingo; this other
'generously lent her time' to Tidy Towns.

What accomplishments might we
attribute to our own housewife,
unless her vigour with the washboard
figured, unless the ill-afforded treats
she brought us from her headscarfed
expeditions to the town, our welcomes home
from school to chops and gravy
dinners, warranted attention?
How she kept her lipsticked dignity
without tap water, bathroom, fridge ...

The page glares back accusingly at us,
blank except for her name, young age,
Valentine's date of death, details
of her 'surviving' husband, children.

Was she an outright failure, therefore,
in the eyes of the world? Had it
no need of further word of her?

Were there no noteworthy deeds to set her
apart from the other 'greatly missed'
mothers in the obit columns?

Had she left no mark whatever
worthy of a record? Miscalculated
so badly as to come to nothing?

Was there no good word we could put in for her?
No persuasive case to be made in her favour?
Could she, our comforter of the afflicted,
have disappeared without a trace?

MEMO TO A PAINTER

Why put so opulent a gloss on the picture
when the unvarnished truth stares you in the face?

Is it not all a bit rich? Why not shame the devil,
tell the story straight, stick to the honest-to-god facts?

Don't fall into the trap of doting parents,
who idolise their babies as some golden calf.

Desist from gilding the lily, over-egging the tempera,
laying a false god before your gallery worshippers.

Every figure witnessed through the stable's
wormy frame was truly humble,

except of course for those slumming visitors
you admit: star-struck kings with gift-wrapped

frankincense and myrrh – odours of sanctity
to offset the noxious fumes of ox and ass –

who kept their distance
from the unkempt shepherds,

the great unwashed whose offering
would morph into a sacrificial lamb,

its horns snagged on the barbed wire
of a crown of thorns.

NOTE: *Adoration of the Magi* ('style of Pieter Coecke van Aelst',
1502–1550), National Gallery of Ireland, depicts the nativity in elegant
surroundings, without the stable or its animals.

2010s

We Irish, born into that ancient sect
But thrown upon this filthy modern tide ...
— W.B. YEATS

How well I remember the early
Twenty Tens, when the Euro-agony
dragged on, chronic depression,
through each recessionary week.

Chancellor Merkel, stern matriarch,
single parent of the EU family,
incredulous at her spendthrift
adolescent dependents,

topped up their pocket money
with Deutschland's life support.
Year by financial year, the credit rating
agencies downgraded Member States,

their loss of boomtime ostentation
as rapid as the toppling
of Arab dictators in those days
of Twitter-fuelled civil coups.

Anti-austerity riots in profligate Spain.
The creaky Greek administration
feeling the heat from workers, hot under
their while collars about abolished perks.

Dissolute Berlusconi jilted in Italy.
Ireland no longer idolising
chummily-named remittance men
it once plied lovingly with landslide polls.

Any gathering of friends could count
on chit-chat punctuated with
'bailouts', 'quantitative easing',
'negative equity', 'debt forgiveness'.

Cries of 'Burn the Bondholders'
went up, like howls for immolation
at the stake: the witch hunt redivivus.
Wall Street occupied. St Paul's Cathedral

grounds monopolised by anti-capitalists:
new scourge of the money changers.
Deep-pile Celtic Tiger fur recycled
as a threadbare hair shirt.

*

We Irish – engulfed in this
filthy tide, protesting our innocence
of every charge – felt confident
of rescue in our hour of need.

Someone was bound
to hasten to our aid;
if not Mother EU, then
our Yankee cousins –

whose ancestors, buried
alive in coffin ships,
fled from famine –
would not see us starve,

Olympic-class charmers that
we are: great *craic*, laid-back,
chancers perhaps – but always
of the most lovable kind;

salt of the earth, adored by everyone,
distinguished by our fetching
snotgreen football kit, toast
of the world in replica Irish bars,

a rebel ballad never far
from our lips, feet responding
in jigtime when a fiddle
strikes the right note.

HOPE ETERNAL

From time to time, the ageing couple
talk of making funeral plans.
But the subject somehow changes.

Now here they are, this Easter,
envisioning the future:
how their savings
may be gobbled up
by eldercare fees,
home monitoring costs,
exorbitant hospital bills.

They warm then to their topic.
Extol medical advances.
Anticipate a further surge
in life expectancy.
Determine to keep fit and well.
Be only as old as they feel.
Maximise the active years ahead.

Hearing them enthuse
you could believe
that someone had
assured them of eternal life.
That they had already
risen from the dead.

GRACE BEFORE MEALS

For what we are about to digest, dear Lord,
our heartfelt thanks. Though you exacted
a hefty price, demanded your pound
of muscular flesh, the sweat and blood

of our furrowed brow, at least you made
due recompense, acknowledged services
accomplished, set blackberries on their marks
for your starting gun, rendered peppers

and tomatoes incandescent, sent apple
blossoms into overdrive, triggered the 'germinate'
function in arable lands, released
pollinators from your strategic bee reserve:

greyhounds darting from a trap.
Let us envision, as we fill voracious plates,
sower, seed, and every food-chain link
to our laden dinner table, from loam-turning

worm to home-delivery grocery bagger,
and not forgetting rain and sun that act
as guarantors that grains, herbs, fruits
and brassica will fulfil their growth potential.

Whether airlifted in burlap sacks imprinted
with a UN logo, slow-cooked as dinner stews
by working couples, picked over on first dates,
or flatbread-wrapped in sidewalk kebab carts,

let us proclaim our thanks for whatever vital
sustenance the philanthropic earth has spared us.
May these compliments to the celestial chef
not fall by the wayside, nor land on barren ground.

GALLERY NUDE

For God's sake,
throw on a dab of paint.
Try to look half-decent.

Take yourself in hand.
Make yourself respectable.
Brush yourself down.

Duck behind the sofa.
Grab that scumbled curtain.
Improvise a fig leaf.

Salvage whatever dignity
you can. You are an
open house, vulnerable

to public scrutiny,
every crevice on full show,
all your flaws laid bare.

Avoid a scandal.
Run for cover.
Wrap up before you start

attracting gawkers.
Let the arty crowd direct
their eyes elsewhere.

IRISH ART AUCTION: THE OLD SCHOOL

Labourers in these milk-and-honey
hayfields neither toil nor spin
but idly while the time away
in spick-and-span landscapes.

Thatched cottages wag a welcoming
tail of smoke. Sunset blazes
a trail to where currachs, lugged
ashore, recover land legs.

These painters adopt
a retrospective line on beauty spots,
return them to the drawing board,
backdate scenic views,

eliminate disfigurement by buildings,
restore fouled lakes to their
pristine state, let them make
a counterpart of sky, match it

cloud for cloud, recast impasto
mountains in watercolour,
soften them up to float
as delicately as leaves.

Drystone walls, plaid-shawled colleens,
hens at large in blossoming orchards,
headstrong horse fairs, donkey creels of peat,
neat villages with window boxes, tea rooms,

lion-mouthed water spouts,
are grist to their riverside mills.
Vistas of little fields mimic
antique Tiffany lampshades.

The sea, though, still holds pride
of place, best-loved of all motifs:
pouted lips of breaking waves,
sheer cliffhangers that, unscathed

from transatlantic journeys,
snap shut on lonesome strands.
And here a pauper's barefoot daughter
tramps a road resurfaced with fresh snows.

Here a flock of plush swans poses.
And, lest old acquaintance be forgot,
a leather-hided ancient, quayside seadog,
puts memories in his pipe and smokes them.

REUNION

With scant regard for privacy,
my parents butt in on my dreams,
cut across my reveries,
abuse my hospitality,
presume on my indulgence
of their unwarranted rebukes,
treat me as a child.

Have they lost all track of time?
Forgotten that we
severed our connection
forty years back?
Are they even conscious
they are dead?

Should I gently break
the bad news, inform them
of their whereabouts,
beg them to keep
to their side of my bed?

4.12

Sleep drops me off
half-way, leaving me
to cope for myself,
complete the journey
into morning under my
own steam, grope back
through clammy blankets
of compacted dark
to the dream house
of childhood I have
just mislaid the key to.

Which way to turn now?
Could that barking mad
racket have been unleashed
by the toy dog
– the miniature collie,
prodigal pet from
the corn flakes packet –
I needed to complete
my full collector's set
of canine breeds?

Arrived at long last,
its agitated scratch
leaves its mark on
what used to be
the front door of
what, once upon
a time, was home.

RED ADMIRAL HIBERNATING

Wings shut for winter business,
the butterfly has come to rest
at our guest-room window ledge:
a striped deckchair stacked away,

folded on the hinges of its wings,
to be dusted off when the sun,
resuscitated, has returned to summer form.
A social butterfly, it lives in quivery

expectation of the next big garden party,
the flower-to-flower flirtation; the ecstasy
of wafting on the trampoline of July heat:
frisky, jittery, shadowboxing, run off its sticky feet.

The very prospect drives a surge of blood
through its piping, illuminates its flight deck,
excitement cramping its juiced-up
abdomen: butterflies-in-the-tummy stuff.

Do not disturb. Tread lightly on its
dreams of buddleia. Home is the sailor.
Home and dry. A Red Sea admiral
returned from voyaging, having

breasted the petalled foam, ridden
the crest of heather waves, triumphed
over predatory enemies, the piratical
rivalry of nectar-guzzling honey bees.

PETITION

With all due deference, Lord,
and whatever kowtowing
your reverence calls for,
we ask for full disclosure
of your strategy, humbly take you
to task for allowing our agony
in your once-paradisal garden
to drag on interminably.
May we appeal for leniency,
touch your bleeding heart,
implore you to weed out
our surplus-to-requirements tribulations.

Restore their rightful memories to Alzheimer patients,
steady the trembling Parkinson's elders,
lift depressives from their vicious torpor,
allow despairing MS victims to step up
nimbly from adjustable beds,
throw off incontinence sheets,
evacuate adapted bathrooms,
dispose of motorised wheelchairs as scrap.

Admit us backstage, permit us access
to your patents, blueprints, R & D,
all the revelations you've denied us,
how you've left us clueless about
the remedy for cancer, groping
for the antidotes to Ebola and flu.

Can we – susceptible to road rage, embezzlement,
ethnic cleansing, schadenfreude –
really be created in your image and likeness?

Or is this your dirty secret: you are no better
than ourselves, no more the Chosen One,
the Great Supreme Commander,
than Kim Jong-il or Chairman Mao,
and – though just as befuddled as
the rest of us about how something
came of nothing – happy to take credit
where not due, brook no dissent,
instigate a crackdown on protestors?

Accept a fault-on-both-sides settlement.
Desist from visiting the sins of our first parents
on us, hellbent though you remain
on vengeance for a fall from grace,
a catastrophic lapse of judgement
that took place aeons before our time.
Good Lord, get over it.
Soften your intransigent stance.
Let the fruits of redemption
be made accessible, tasted wholly:
the perks of your breathtaking escapade,
your daredevil suspense story,
your born-again plotline
of death and resurrection;
a three-day wonder that exerts
a mesmerising grip on our imaginations still,
a fascination that translates
into big-budget films, church fêtes,
cult followings, inhuman civil wars.

CHRISTMAS IDYLL

And after a duvet-wrappered
lie-in, to find all the standard
props reliably in place: a silver pot
of hot-shot coffee miniaturising
the log fire blaze; exotic chocolates
from a son's adopted country;
mince pies; mulled wine; vintage
TV comedy; fried breakfast –
everything permitted for a day,
all dietary restrictions lifted.

There too, in the rarely-inhabited
sitting room, carols, crackers, balloons,
shimmering tinsel garlands, a card-
sprouting tree aglow with excitement,
sharing the delight of those whose
gifts it nurtures like laid eggs.
No tension in the air yet. No old
resentments flaring yet among
the children, each on best behaviour,
home with studded boyfriends, urbane,
designer-attired young wives.

How precious they must look from
the empty street, framed picture-perfect
between chintzy curtains, untouched
by suffering, immune from pain,
luxuriating in an otherworldly Thursday
that segues to a dreamy Sunday.

Only the clock-watching woman
coaxing the stove in the lonely
flagstoned kitchen – fretting over
dinner preparations, rinsing sprouts,
basting turkey, struggling to recover
a duck pâté gone wrong –
maintains a foothold in real time.

Stepping out to bin the forcemeat
waste, add roast potato peelings
to the compost heap, she is assailed
by melancholic winds, whipped
by hail, chilled by a dark killjoy air
that – refusing even a single
day's remission – threatens
to rough up this stage set,
snuff out the frivolous fairy lights,
abolish the nonsense
of a goodwill season,
pour cold water on the fire,
bring down the whole house
of glitzy greeting cards,
drown out the ethereal boy treble's
tidings of *comfort and joy,*
comfort and joy, expose a raw
world incapable of betterment:
our dusty futures hanging on
the prospects of a small blue
planetary bauble in a glittering,
infinitely expanding universe.

UPDATE

God, I still miss you some days,
fondly recall our happier times.
You used to take me into
your confidence, while I
fessed up to my transgressions,
owned up to grievous flaws.
And, granted absolution, I would
ascend to cloud nine,
mind on higher things,
ears only for your voice that conversed,
not in our inarticulate vernacular
but through lapidary Latin,
plainchant, exultant motet.
I recall the wet cathedral evenings
when your fair-weather friends
had absented themselves,
and we settled down by the fire
of the votive candle shrine
for a heart-to-heart confab,
our conversation never flagging.

What a good listener you always were
to me, God. I so wish we had not quarrelled,
gone our separate ways, making
too big an issue of the Jesuitical
distinctions that divided us, failing
to see eye-to-eye on articles of faith.

I still watch out for news of you,
gossip column tattle, and – an obsessive
divorcee – track your movements, eager
to learn which lovers take my place,

what types you hang about with these days,
what you're up to elsewhere
as you expand your horizons,
establishing new branches of your empire,
propagating universes by the second.

And you must feel a loneliness
close to empty nest syndrome
now that so many of your
erstwhile acolytes have flown the coop,
escaped your cage, questioned
your discretion, no longer prepared
to submit to your rough justice,
remain prisoners of your conscience.

God, how much I miss the comfort food
of your home-baked communion host.
And hush. The megaphones roped
to the telegraph poles relay around
the town your May procession:
The blue-gowned Child of Mary
women join with the choir.
The petal-strewing schoolgirls,
the banner-carrying sodality men,
and the canopy-bearing deacons
– custodians of the fragile Marian shrine
buoyant on its wildflower-brimming float –
break into song, give 'full-throated' voice
to the humming fecundity of early summer.

The year, refurbished, kitted out afresh,
is soaking up warm pastel colours,
reaching perfect pitch, oozing
through rejuvenated fields
a slow sempiternal note.

BEDTIME

No smoke without fire: ash droppings,
flashing cigarette morse from the other
brass bed, give my uncle's whereabouts away.

He is plotting his tomorrows before sleep:
install tripods for peas, weed the mangolds,
turn further hay for winter's feeding frenzy.

The small sash window, crouching under dapper
thatch, is open wide, scouting for a breath of air,
our tartan Foxford blankets thrown overboard.

Day's over-eager light does not know when
to stop: I can still speedread wallpaper rosebuds,
bear witness to the holy pictures' apparitions.

A Beauty of Bath apple ferment overwhelms
the back room, where pheasants slump from
doors in autumn, and vital supplies are stored:

plump beer-bellied Guinness bottles and Time ale
for visitors; Corcoran's orangeade; selection boxes
of Lemon's Pure Sweets for grandchildren;

jelly and custard leftovers; canned mandarin oranges
and fruit cocktail; Goodall's salad cream; beetroot-red
sandwich meat; skinless sausages; flaking grinder loaves..

Little flutterings and scurryings from the farmyard.
Then everything settles again. I wake to a grainy smell –
the boiling vat of layers' mash – dinging churns,

uncles up, about in overalls, and singing, from their milking stools, 'Lipstick on Your Collar', or 'Achin' Breakin' Heart', to boost the friesians' creamy yield.

ABOUT THE AUTHOR

Born in Thurles, County Tipperary, in 1954, Dennis O'Driscoll published eight previous books of poetry, including *New and Selected Poems* (Anvil Press, 2004), a Poetry Book Society Special Commendation, and *Reality Check* (Copper Canyon Press, 2008), shortlisted for the Irish Times / Poetry Now Prize 2008. A selection of his essays and reviews, *Troubled Thoughts, Majestic Dreams* (Gallery Press), was published in 2001. He edited a book of contemporary quotations about poetry, *Quote Poet Unquote* (Copper Canyon Press, 2008), and his book *Stepping Stones: Interviews with Seamus Heaney* (Farrar, Straus and Giroux) was published in 2008; it was shortlisted for 'Book of the Decade' in the Irish Book Awards 2010.

Among numerous anthologies in which his work *appears are The Penguin Book of Irish Poetry, An Anthology of Modern Irish Poetry* (Harvard University Press), *20th Century Irish Poems* (Faber) and *Poetry* magazine's anthology (Ivan R. Dee). A substantial selection of his work is included in *The Wake Forest Series of Irish Poetry 1* (Wake Forest University Press, 2005).

Poetry is vital to language and living. Since 1972, Copper Canyon Press has published extraordinary poetry from around the world to engage the imaginations and intellects of readers, writers, booksellers, librarians, teachers, students, and donors.

WE ARE GRATEFUL FOR THE MAJOR SUPPORT PROVIDED BY:

THE PAUL G. ALLEN
FAMILY FOUNDATION

CULTURE

Lannan

National
Endowment
for the Arts
arts.gov
ART WORKS.

OFFICE OF ARTS & CULTURE
SEATTLE

WE ARE GRATEFUL FOR THE MAJOR SUPPORT PROVIDED BY:

Anonymous

John Branch

Diana Broze

Beroz Ferrell & The Point, LLC

Janet and Les Cox

Mimi Gardner Gates

Linda Gerrard and Walter Parsons

Gull Industries, Inc.
on behalf of William and Ruth True

Mark Hamilton and Suzie Rapp

Carolyn and Robert Hedin

Steven Myron Holl

Lakeside Industries, Inc.
on behalf of Jeanne Marie Lee

Maureen Lee and Mark Busto

Brice Marden

Ellie Mathews and Carl Youngmann
as The North Press

H. Stewart Parker

Penny and Jerry Peabody

John Phillips and Anne O'Donnell

Joseph C. Roberts

Cynthia Lovelace Sears and
Frank Buxton

The Seattle Foundation

Kim and Jeff Seely

David and Catherine Eaton Skinner

Dan Waggoner

C.D. Wright and Forrest Gander

Charles and Barbara Wright

The dedicated interns and faithful volunteers
of Copper Canyon Press

~~~~~

TO LEARN MORE ABOUT UNDERWRITING COPPER CANYON PRESS TITLES,
PLEASE CALL 360-385-4925 EXT. 103

The Chinese character for poetry is made up of two parts:
"word" and "temple." It also serves as pressmark for
Copper Canyon Press.